EUROPEAN COACHES IN BRITAIN

MALCOLM BATTEN

AMBERLEY

First published 2024

Amberley Publishing
The Hill, Stroud
Gloucestershire, GL5 4EP

www.amberley-books.com

ISBN 978 1 3981 1845 4 (print)
ISBN 978 1 3981 1846 1 (ebook)

British Library Cataloguing in Publication Data.
A catalogue record for this book is available from the British Library.

Typesetting by Hurix Digital, India.
Printed in the UK.

Introduction

Nowadays, the European coach market is dominated by a few manufacturers whose products are sold across the Continent and beyond – think Mercedes-Benz, Iveco, Scania, Volvo, etc. Some of these vehicles are integrals such as the products of Neoplan and Setra, with the body and mechanical units constructed together rather than as separate units. Others will be sold as a chassis, which may come with either bodywork by the chassis maker or by one of a number of bodybuilders whose products are again sold right across Europe and beyond. As well as European-owned manufacturers, there is considerable input from China and Japan.

It wasn't always like this. From the end of the Second World War until the late 1960s, virtually all buses and coaches bought by British operators were British-made. Similarly, many European countries had chassis makers whose products were sold primarily within that country or to neighbours without a maker of their own. Thus, there was Berliet and Saviem from France, Büssing from Germany, Fiat from Italy, etc. Where these were separate chassis, they would be bodied by a range of local bodybuilders within each country, again mainly supplying a domestic market. Britain was desperate to export in order to repay our wartime debts to the USA, and British chassis were sold to some European markets, especially Greece, Holland and Portugal. Elsewhere, British-designed AEC and Leyland engines and mechanical units formed the basis of products constructed under licence and marketed under local names such as Sisu in Finland and DAB in Denmark.

Until the 1960s, it was rare for European coaches to enter Britain as they would need to be craned aboard a ship and carried as deck cargo. The introduction of roll-on/roll-off ferries changed this. A few were brought over and appeared at the British Coach Rally at Brighton as early as 1959, when a Setra from Germany and a Scania-Vabis from Holland contrasted with the sixty-six British-built and owned coaches. These British vehicles included twelve Bedford SB3s with petrol engines. In 1963, of fifty-two coaches entered there was one foreign entry – a Fiat from Italy. In 1964 there were six foreign entries amongst the eighty-one that took part, although from 1965 to 1968 there were none.

When Britain entered the Common Market (later European Community) in 1972, this facilitated and encouraged tourism, which took off in a big way. Increasing numbers of visitors came from Europe including by coach. Car ferries from British Rail Sealink, Townsend Thoresen, Brittany Ferries and DFDS, amongst others, brought in the vehicles. Simplified standard control documentation with fifteen European countries was also agreed from 1 April 1972 for public-service vehicles on 'closed door tours' travelling to or from these countries. Later, in 1977 *Buses* magazine reported on a marked increase in European coaches visiting Britain for Queen Elizabeth II's Silver Jubilee celebrations.

Many of these European coach designs seemed quite exotic compared with the home-produced products. There were three-axle coaches when such vehicles were not found here (other than the twin-steer Bedford VAL). There were double-deck Neoplan and Setra coaches from Germany, and even some articulated coaches. Many body designs had larger windows and more chrome work than was the norm here. Some of the liveries, especially from Germany, became quite elaborate with airbrushed designs applied to them. Some coaches pulled luggage trailers. Occasionally you could see the really bizarre-looking 'hotel coaches' that included sleeping accommodation.

Some of the company names were quite fascinating. There was a Belgian company called Jovial Car – they must have been a jolly lot! Then there was the intriguingly named 'Spies Reisen' – a case of hiding in plain sight perhaps?

Later, the collapse of the Iron Curtain from November 1989 onwards, and the subsequent entry of former Eastern European countries to the EC, brought in a new source of visitors. It also brought vehicle makes even less familiar to British eyes, such as Karosa from the Czech Republic and Jelcz and Autosan from Poland. The opening of the Channel Tunnel in May 1994 provided an alternative form of access to the ferries, although these remain the prime route for coaches.

The 1991 Transport & Road Research Laboratory report *Tourist Coaches in London* noted coaches from twenty foreign countries, of which 70 per cent were from France and Germany.

Of course, it wasn't just one-way traffic. British coach operators started offering tours to Europe. Amongst the leaders in this field were Wallace Arnold of Leeds and Excelsior European Motorways of Bournemouth. The latter even offered tours to Moscow in the 1960s following a proving run in 1959 when the Iron Curtain was still firmly in place. South-coast bus companies including East Kent and Southdown also had extensive coaching fleets and offered European tours from the 1960s.

In June 1968 *Buses* magazine reported on a new company, Watts International, running a service from London to Athens with an AEC Reliance coach. By 1974 National Bus Company fleet National Travel South East was working a London–Frankfurt service, which in 1974 had one journey a week extended to Athens. This was operated as part of the Europabus network and within Europe was worked in conjunction with Deutsche Touring Gesellschaft and Belgian company L'Epervier. However, through working to Britain by European operators did not begin until 1975, when the use of left-hand-drive vehicles on such services was legalised on British roads. In 1976 National Express began a Cheltenham–Paris service, and it was also in 1976 that National Travel South East bought four left-hand-drive AEC Reliance coaches for European work. Services were considerably expanded for the 1979 season with National Express, Grey-Green Coaches and Wallace Arnold from Britain working with a number of European partners to provide through services or connections to many countries throughout Western Europe.

Foreign entry to the British coach market in the 1960s began at the 1966 Commercial Motor Show at Earls Court when Mercedes-Benz exhibited a right-hand-drive version of their 0302 integral coach, although this did not meet the British regulations in place at that time. A fully compatible model was shown at the 1968 show. Meanwhile, an 0302 demonstrator registered OLH 302E was tried out by several operators in 1967, including by Sheffield United Tours on their Sheffield–Blackpool express service. This coach was then sold to Whiteford, Lanark, in 1968. Seamarks, Luton, bought the 1968 show vehicle, then another and ordered five more in 1969. Earlier in 1966, Eastern Scottish gained special dispensation to try out a German-built Magirus Deutz 10-metre left-hand-drive coach on the Edinburgh–London service. It was given registration GFS 948D during its stay. At the 1968 Commercial Motor Show there was also a German-built Büssing Prafekt 15 coach shown in the demonstration park. More significantly, the dealer Alf Moseley of Loughborough began marketing the 'Moseley Continental' coachwork built by Salvador Caetano of Portugal and had an example of their Lisboa model on a Leyland Leopard chassis that had been sold to R&S Travel of London.

The European makers exhibited their wares not only at the Commercial Motor Shows but also at the Blackpool and Brighton coach rallies, which acted as trade shows by and for the coaching industry. At Brighton in 1969 there were five coaches with Caetano coachwork, four on Bedford chassis and one on a Leyland chassis. There were seven Caetano-bodied coaches in 1970 and twelve in 1971. Moseley later offered other makes of European bodywork, including Unicar of Spain and Autokori of Finland. Only two Autokori bodies came to the UK – SYD 86M for Arleen, Bath, in 1973 and GKM 406N for Sonners, Rainham, Kent, in 1974. Both were on Bedford YRQ chassis.

As an alternative to the integral 0302, Mercedes-Benz offered the model as a chassis sub-frame fitted with a Plaxton Panorama Elite C48F body at the Scottish Motor Show, Glasgow, in 1969. At the smaller end of the market, Williams Motor Group of Manchester offered their Deansgate sixteen-seat coach body conversion on the Mercedes-Benz L406D Transporter van from 1969, exhibiting at the Blackpool and Brighton coach rallies.

The first European companies to break through into the British commercial-vehicle market had been the Swedish chassis makers Scania and Volvo, whose lorries started to sell in the UK from 1967, with coaches coming in the 1970s. This was due to Britain and Sweden both being members of EFTA, the European Free Trade Association. Volvo invested heavily in export marketing from 1969 onwards and opened a new bus and coach chassis plant at Boras, Sweden, in 1977. Indeed, in 1977 87 per cent of their production was for export. Their B58 coach chassis found a ready market in Britain from its introduction in 1973, reaching a total of 1,294 sold by 1982, when it was replaced by the B10M, first introduced in 1980. Scania formed a joint venture with Metro-Cammell Weymann in 1969, which led to the Metro-Scania buses from 1971. They brought an experimental CR145 coach with a 260-bhp V8 rear-mounted engine to Britain in 1973, which was tried by National Express but won no orders. After the end of the joint venture in 1979, they re-entered the market on their own in 1980, with coaches on offer from 1982. Britain's entry to the Common Market in 1972 opened the doors to companies from other member countries to market their products here, such as DAF from Holland.

When British coach companies started to offer tours to Europe, they found that British coaches were comparatively underpowered and less suited to autobahns and steep mountain roads than European chassis. When Leyland introduced the Tiger chassis in 1981 to replace the 180-bhp Leopard it initially had a 218-bhp TL11H engine, but this was quickly supplemented by a 245-bhp model and a turbocharged 260-bhp model to compete with the contemporary competition from the Volvo B10M (230 bhp), DAF MB200 (251 bhp), etc.

European-built coach bodies and integrals were generally more expensive than British equivalents so did not catch on extensively at first. There was also a distrust of integrals as not being the British norm. But these vehicles were higher specified. Facilities such as toilets and catering provision were not regularly provided on British-built vehicles as comfort/refreshment breaks en route were the norm. Neither was air conditioning, although this was far more prevalent in hotter countries such as Italy and Spain. But for Continental touring these became more relevant and so some upmarket companies invested in such vehicles. Later in the early 1980s, British companies bought European integrals as a short-lived boom in coach shuttles to tourist destinations and winter-sports resorts developed. Probably the ready availability of spares and mechanical support in Europe may have been one factor in this. High-floor integrals and double-deck coaches became popular with their increased luggage capacity for skis and other equipment. Some of these vehicles might be notching up some 5,000 miles a week with almost non-stop travel.

Deregulation of UK long-distance coach services in 1980 brought competition to National Express from a number of independent operators trading initially under the short-lived British Coachways banner, then later in collaboration with National Express. New faster services with refreshments served on board were introduced by both parties, the National Express response being marketed as 'Rapide'. One of these new services was started by Trathens of Yelverton, between Plymouth, Exeter and London (Gloucester Road) non-stop in four hours. For this they bought the first two Neoplan Skyliner double-deck coaches for a British operator in 1981.

Another market being increasingly captured by the Europeans was for so-called high specification 'executive' coaches, operated as football club team coaches and for use by touring pop groups.

By the early 1980s European-built or bodied coaches could be found in all types of fleets, from municipalities to the National Bus Company, the Scottish Bus Group and independents. As well as touring work, they could be found on National Express and Scottish Citylink services, commuter services such as Southend Transport's from Southend to London and (from 1984) Green Line airport link services. For a while there were also some rare combinations of European engines and bodywork on British-made chassis. For instance, NBC fleet Yorkshire Traction refitted some Leyland Leopard coaches with DAF engines in 1984, whilst fellow NBC fleet East Kent had some AEC Reliance coaches rebodied by Berkhof. The switch to European-built coaches into the 1980s can perhaps best be appreciated by the fact that at the 1982 British Coach Rally at Brighton forty-two entries were all British, whilst forty-one were either entirely foreign or on foreign chassis. The Coach of the Year award went to a Setra executive coach VAV 1X with tables, toilet, etc., for Kenzie's, Shepreth.

At the 1982 Motor Show held at the Birmingham National Exhibition Centre, Leyland Bus did not even exhibit. There were new British-made coach chassis from Dennis and MCW, joining the hotly contested market with a host of Continental makes including Scania showing a coach chassis, the K112 range, for the first time in the UK.

The choice of British-made chassis declined in the 1980s with both Ford and Bedford having ceased production by 1986, leaving only Dennis supplying the lightweight market. In March 1988 it was announced that Leyland Bus Group, sold to its management in 1987, had now been acquired by Volvo. Leyland models would become either phased out or marketed as Volvos into the 1990s. The Leyland plant was closed and production, including that of Volvo B10M chassis, was concentrated at Workington until that too closed in 1993. Vehicles were then made at Volvo's plant at Irvine until that also closed in 2000, when production for the UK market was switched to Sweden.

As the European Union expanded, the main manufacturers became more pan-European, opening plants in various countries, not only in Europe. For instance, by the end of 1991 Scania was the world's fourth largest truck manufacturer with plants in fourteen countries on five continents. The smaller local makers and bodybuilders were absorbed and disappeared, leaving the global brands we see today.

In this book, I look back at the variety of vehicles from a wide range of makers and bodybuilders that came to Britain from all over Europe between the 1970s and early 2000s. Living in London, I saw and photographed many such vehicles. There were certain locations that were prime spots for foreign vehicles. These included the coach park at St Paul's Cathedral (now closed), Park Lane and a coach park by Gloucester Road station, which was later closed down after locals complained that it was being used as a coach station without having planning permission for that purpose. The old St Pancras goods station site, now home to the British Library, was also used as a coach park-cum-coach station *c.* 1979–81, including by the short-lived British Coachways consortium. The coach park at Windsor was and remains another excellent location for photographing foreign (and British) coaches.

The number of visiting coaches declined from the 1990s, as a result of the Channel Tunnel and the emergence of budget airlines serving London City Airport and expanded facilities at Luton, Stanstead, etc. Although there were still several vehicles from the nearest countries – France, Belgium, Germany, Holland and Spain – those from further afield became rarer.

The worldwide Covid pandemic put an end to the influx of European tourists, and despite the relaxation and lifting of restrictions, the number of visiting coaches nowhere returned to previous levels. On a weekend visit to Windsor in June 2022 there were just three coaches in the coach park, only one of which was foreign owned. It has picked up some more in 2023, perhaps boosted by the TV coverage of the Coronation of King Charles III.

Also included in the book are some of the vehicles used on the early international coach services from London, and some of the early examples of foreign-built chassis, bodies and integrals bought by British companies from *c.* 1970 to the early 1980s.

All photographs are by the author.

European Visiting Coaches by Country

Austria

Coaches from Austria were quite a rarity in London and this is a typical German-built Neoplan N122 double-decker, but with the addition of a luggage trailer. This was seen opposite St Paul's Cathedral in August 1983.

Belgium

The European Cup Final match at Wembley Stadium on 10 May 1978 between Liverpool FC and Club Brugge of Belgium brought a wide selection of coaches from Belgium. Royal Tours, Ostend, sent a number of these Bus & Car Eagle coaches. This one was more interesting than most as it sports Hoverlloyd livery. It was presumably used for a service connecting with the Hoverlloyd hovercraft service from Ramsgate to Calais (see also p. 75).

A more recent Bus & Car Eagle design stands in front of the old Wembley Stadium. Built in Brugge (Bruges), the styling was similar to American practice. This was no coincidence as Bus & Car had its origins in Kässbohrer (Setra) of Germany, who designed and built coaches for the American Continental Trailways Company from 1955 to 1958. When Kässbohrer decided to concentrate on the European market, Continental teamed up with a Belgian company La Brugeoise to build the next generation of coaches based on the Setra designs as Bus & Car and they also built for the European market until production ended in 1980. To the left is a Lancia, an Italian chassis make more associated with cars.

Retie Cars, from Retie, sent this DAF with Jonckheere C50F coachwork. This Belgian company was established in the nineteenth century and by the 1980s over 85 per cent of production from the factory at Roeselare was exported. The company was taken over by the Dutch company Berkhof in 1994 but they retained their separate names.

A Dutch-built Bova coach working for Omnium Tours. Taken at Gloucester Road coach park, London, in August 1980.

Ramoudt Tours, Ostend, owned this DAF with bodywork by the Belgian company LAG, which was taken at St Paul's Cathedral in April 1981. This style of LAG bodywork, known as the Galaxy model, was first offered in the UK through dealers Yeates of Loughborough in 1982, with Harry Shaw Coaches of Coventry being one of the first customers.

A Fiat with Van Hool bodywork seen in London, June 1982. In January 1975 Fiat, OM and Lancia of Italy merged with Unic of France and Magirus Deutz of Germany to form Iveco (Industrial Vehicles Corporation). In 1980 Magirus Deutz sold their share in the company to Fiat, making it a fully Italian-owned business. Van Hool of Belgium first began in 1947 and remains a major builder of both integral coaches and separate bodywork, as well as trailers. However, they became bankrupt in 2024 and the bus part of the business was sold to VDL of Holland.

Czech Republic

Ceskoslovenská Státni Automobilová Doprava (CSAD), Prague, with a typical Karosa LC735 integral, seen at Gloucester Road in June 1985. Karosa had their origins in a company founded by Josef Sodomka in 1899 that built car bodies. Under Communism, the company was nationalised in 1948, renamed Karosa and became the sole makers of buses and coaches in Czechoslovakia. The LC735 model was made from 1983 to 1991.

A later-style Karosa of CSAD Rosice seen in Park Lane, April 1995.

This Karosa was the LC936 model built from 1996 to 2002. This was also taken in Park Lane, this time in April 1998. In 1994 Karosa had been bought into by Renault and the Renault diamond badge is also mounted on the front.

Another Karosa taken at St Paul's Cathedral in August 1996. In 1999 Karosa became part of Irisbus, a pan-European venture formed by Renault and Iveco. Iveco took over the whole business in 2003 and from 2007 the Karosa name was dropped in favour of Iveco Bus. The plant is the largest bus manufacturing factory in Europe.

An Oasa body was mounted on this coach photographed at Windsor, May 1996.

Denmark

This old Scania-Vabis, probably dating from the early 1950s, was being used as a mobile caravan when seen in February 1975.

A pair of elderly Volvo coaches with unknown bodywork parked up in Bayswater, London, in June 1977. They were owned by a company called Kvidbjerg Harup from Thisted, Denmark.

This is Svends Turistfart of Silkeborg with a Mercedes-Benz that has a thirty-five-seat body by Saro Karosserifabrik. Taken in June 1978.

Something more modern, this is Nils Juels Bussar, Ikast, with a Scania that has a Petersen C42F body. Petersen were based at Herning in Denmark. Taken at St Paul's Cathedral, February 1982.

Leyland DAB was a Danish subsidiary of Leyland Motors, later British Leyland. This DAB with DAB bodywork was No. 4 in the fleet of Tarm Rute and Turistfart. With its large blind box, it is what we would call a dual-purpose design in Britain – equally suited for long-distance bus work or coaching when required. A similar design vehicle was exhibited at the 1980 Commercial Motor Show held at the National Exhibition Centre, Birmingham, but there were no British orders. After the collapse of Leyland, DAB became part of the United Bus Group as DAB-Silkeborg AS and was then acquired by Scania in 1994, who sold it on in 2001.

British-made Plaxton bodywork won some export orders to Europe. This Plaxton Paramount 3500 body is mounted on a DAF SB3000 chassis and was with Danish operator Brdr Kolsen when photographed at Windsor in June 1995. Over 100 Plaxton bodies were sold to Denmark between 1975 and 1980 on a variety of chassis makes.

This three-axle MAN seen at Brighton in May 2006 was with Centrumturist from Arhus.

Particularly interesting is this Scania with Finnish-built Delta Plan bodywork seen at Windsor in July 1994. The registration indicates that this comes from the Faroe Islands, an autonomous part of the Kingdom of Denmark with a total population of a little over 50,000. It must have had quite an interesting journey to get from there to the UK.

Estonia

Seen at Windsor in June 1995, this is a Mercedes-Benz with bodywork by Delta Plan of Finland. Estonia became independent in August 1991, and being directly opposite Finland across the Gulf of Finland, many vehicles began to be imported from there to replace the Communist-era vehicles.

Also at Windsor in July 1999 is this Scania of Skorpian PJ. The bodywork is also probably of Scandinavian origin.

Finland

Belonging to F. Myllymäki of Tampere, this is a Scania 116 with Ajokki integral C49F bodywork. This was at St Paul's in May 1982. Ajokki was founded in Tampere in 1942 and acquired Delta Plan in 1982.

Suomen Touristauto Oy, Helsinki, No. 306, a Volvo with Delta Plan C45F bodywork, in January 1982. This company had begun as Autokori in 1936 and was based at Turku. In 1973 they moved to Lieto and soon after changed their name to Delta Plan.

Also with Delta Plan bodywork is this Mercedes-Benz of Kyttälä Star seen in July 1986. As stated above, Delta Plan was acquired by Ajokki in 1982. In 1986 Ajokki came into common ownership with Wiima, which in 1989 became Carrus. Carrus became a Volvo subsidiary in 1997, becoming Volvo Bus Finland in 2004. It then reverted to Finnish ownership as Carrus Delta in 2008.

Tep Tour were the owners of this Scania with bodywork by Kutter from Helsinki, parked up in Park Lane, October 1995. Note that this is towing a luggage trailer.

This Scania CR111 also has Kutter bodywork and belonged to Laurilan Linja Oy, Helsinki. This was parked in Colchester bus station in July 1983.

LEC 288 is a Volvo with bodywork by Lahti. Owned by Ylisuvanto Oy, it was parked in May 1983 on what is now the site of the British Library in Euston Road, formerly St Pancras goods yard and at the time being used as a coach park. Lahden Autokori started making buses and coaches at Lahti in 1967 with most production until 2007 being for the home market. They then built coaches for Scania until 2013, when the factory was closed with Scania moving production to Poland where labour costs were lower.

Pulling out of the coach park at St Paul's Cathedral is a Volvo with Wiima bodywork from Mikko Rindell of Turku. It is interesting how many of the Finnish coaches were painted in the national flag colours of blue and white and displayed the flag on their paintwork.

France

A Berliet of Andre Deschanel, Jussey, seen in May 1979. Marius Berliet began car production in 1895 and commercial vehicles including buses from 1907. Berliet was acquired by Renault in 1975.

A rather unusual forward-control Berliet midi coach pulls out of Horse Guards Parade on 25 June 1977. This was with Cars Autin of Arque-le-Bataille.

A Saviem of Scal Voyages, taken at Windsor in June 1980. Saviem was an acronym for Société Anonyme de Véhicules Industriels et d'Équipements Méchaniques. They were formed in 1955 by a merger of Renault's heavy vehicle production with Somua and Latil. In 1959 they became a full subsidiary of Renault.

A different model from Saviem seen at Victoria in April 1980. In 1978 Saviem was merged with Berliet, which had been acquired by Renault in 1975, and in 1980 the separate marque names were dropped in favour of Renault.

At the same location in April 1982 is a Renault PR14 of Voyages Suzanne, Evreux. Renault had first started building commercial vehicles in 1909 and were unusual for the time for using shaft drive from the start rather than chain drive.

Seen at St Paul's in May 1983, this Renault is fitted with an Irizar body, built in Spain. It features a slightly raised rear section, a feature popular with a number of body designers during this period. This was with Jardel Tourisme, Montaubon.

A Belgian-built three-axle Bus & Car Eagle of Tourisme Verney, Lyon, in July 1983. This was at the Battersea coach park used mainly by National Express vehicles on layover.

Also with Tourisme Verney were a number of these three-axle CBM (Car et Bus Le Mans) Albatross coaches. These had unusual styling with a very flat front that slopes forward towards the top. They were powered by a Mercedes-Benz V8 engine. Taken in Gloucester Road, May 1986.

This is a Gruaudaf. I believe this was a collaboration between the French company Gruau and DAF. The vehicles were built at Chantilly. Taken at Battersea, September 1984.

Seen at Windsor in May 1986 is a Unic of Cars Ouest Acquitain, St Medard. Unic became part of Iveco (Industrial Vehicles Corporation) when this was formed in 1975, and I photographed similar coaches badged as Iveco. Bodywork was by Carosserie Lorraine, another subsidiary of Iveco, which was later sold to British coachbuilders Plaxton in 1989, but subsequently closed in 1992.

Autocars Roger brought over this Scania 86 with coachwork by Dutch makers Den Oudsten, seen at Gloucester Road in March 1982. Den Oudsten had 70 per cent of the Dutch service-bus-body market when they were taken over by United Bus BV, a grouping that included DAF and Bova in 1990. This grouping collapsed in 1993 and the Den Oudsten family bought the company back in 1994. However, a fall in orders led to the company going bankrupt in 2001.

This Magirus Deutz taken in London in May 1983 was noted as having bodywork by Chardom.

This Renault has rather square-looking Carrier bodywork. This was seen at Taunton, Somerset, in June 1988 and belonged to Voyages Michel, Vern D'Anjou.

The Renault Tracer model was produced from 1991 to 2001, with a horizontal underfloor Renault engine and a dual-purpose style of body. It was announced at the time that separate underframes would be made available for local bodybuilders in other countries, which could include Britain. This Tracer of Marne et Morin was seen in Park Lane during June 1996.

Germany

The oldest vehicle from Germany I encountered was this rear-engined Büssing with KraussMaffei bodywork, which was at Battersea in August 1975. This was not with a German coach company but, as the Union Jack flags hint, was actually with the British Army of the Rhine. KraussMaffei also used to manufacture railway and military equipment but by the 1980s had specialised in injection moulding machines for the plastics industry.

A Büssing of Verkehtsbetriebe Bachstein, Hornberg, at Bayswater in September 1978. This had only forty-one well-spaced seats. Büssing was established in 1903 with buses first produced in 1904 at their works in Braunschweig. Büssing was taken over by MAN in 1971, who have continued to utilise the Büssing lion symbol as their badge.

A Büssing integral at Gloucester Road in September 1981. Note the former Royal Blue Bristol RELH/ECW alongside.

A MAN of Vehling, Bergkamen, at Gloucester Road in September 1985. MAN stands for Maschinenfabrik Augsburg Nurnberg.

The products of Setra are still being made but are now rather more exotic than this S120 design seen visiting Oxford back in 1971. Seating forty-one, it was owned by Bus-Verkehr Omnibus-Betriebs of Berlin. Setra integrals were first manufactured by Karl Kässbohrer of Ulm, Germany, in 1950 and in 1983 they delivered their 35,000th coach. The name Setra was derived from the German words '*selbst tragend*', meaning self-supporting, and they also built coaches for Continental Trailways in the USA (see p. 9). Kässbohrer was taken over by Daimler-Benz in January 1995 to form EvoBus, but the Setra range and name were retained along with the Mercedes-Benz name.

Parked up outside the entrance to London Zoo in April 1976 is this Magirus Deutz fifty-three-seat coach of Adammer Reisen, Schloss Holte. Behind is a Plaxton-bodied coach from Trent in the now standard National coach white livery. Magirus Deutz, from Ulm, became part of Iveco in 1975 but the name was retained into the 1980s. The Magirus name is now only used for their firefighting vehicles.

This Magirus Deutz might be considered as a having a dual-purpose body style with its unused blind box above the windscreen, but there are curtains at the windows for a touch of luxury appeal. Photographed in October 1985.

This Mercedes-Benz of Pier-Huwe Reisen, Coesfeld, seen in May 1981, has two doors, fifty-three seats and dual-purpose bodywork (i.e. DP53D). Mercedes-Benz dates back to 1926 when the companies of Karl Benz and Gottlieb Daimler merged and now have factories on several continents and are the largest brand of premium vehicles in the world. '*Sonderfahrt*' means 'special excursion'.

Designed to impress, who could resist touring in this superb Mercedes-Benz 0302 with its raised seating, the company name in cast letters above the windscreen and the names of major European capital cities emblazoned on the sides. It is seen parked outside Victoria Coach Station in September 1985. The bodywork was by Vetter and it had forty-six seats. The owners were Libhöfer's Reisen of Bochum.

Taken at Gloucester Road in April 1981, this Mercedes-Benz of HDC Reisen, Duisberg, has bodywork by Ernst Auwärter. Their models had 'Star' names and this was the Eurostar, a name in use long before the Channel Tunnel opened in 1994! A Setra S215H integral coach is alongside.

Stylish, simple clean lines on this Vetter body mounted on a Mercedes-Benz 0303 chassis, July 1983. Introduced in 1974, the 0303 would be become the world's most successful coach, selling over 35,000 worldwide as chassis or integral vehicles before replacement by the 0404 model in 1992. Of these, a total of 223 were sold to British companies.

Mercedes-Benz minibuses and minicoaches would become common in Britain from the mid-1980s onwards. This example from Rymsa-Reisen, Dortmund, has twenty-nine-seat Ernst Auwärter bodywork. Ernst Auwärter came from a family business dating back to 1854 that included making bus bodies from 1928. He separated to specialise in coaches from 1949. In later years small minicoaches and buses were a speciality. The company eventually went bankrupt in 2005 following foreign competition and declining sales. Taken at St Paul's Cathedral, March 1980.

A classic example of the Neoplan Skyliner double-deck coach. Neoplan was founded by Gottlob Auwärter, a brother of Ernst, at Stuttgart in 1935 and by 1953 had developed integral coaches rather than separate bodywork. The double-deck Skyliner was first introduced in 1964. Those panoramic windows curving up into the roofline would be ideal for touring through the mountain scenery. This example at St Pancras in August 1983 was with Niebäumer of Bad Salzuflen, a spa resort in North Rhine-Westphalia.

Although this is also badged as a Neoplan Skyliner, the bodywork on this is more restrained. The windows are smaller and do not extend into the roofline. There are also windows with sliding opening sections rather than the vehicle being air-conditioned. Trafalgar Square, April 1994.

Neoplan didn't just make the Skyliner double-deckers. This short coach shares the windscreen style and curved panoramic windows. It was owned by a company from Weissenthurm, a town about 12 km north-west of Koblenz. August 1983.

This stylish twenty-four-seat midicoach is also a Neoplan and is the N907 model. This example, seen in April 1988, was with Veelker, Gronau. The first example of this model to be bought by a British company went to Duckworth, Gisburn, in 1982 and was fitted with a MAN engine and twenty-three reclining seats.

Ideal Reisen, Kreuztal, entered this new Setra S228DT Imperial double-deck coach at the 1983 British Coach Rally at Brighton, where it was the winner of several awards. A left-hand-drive version had been shown at the 1982 Motor Show. The first UK customer would be Carnell, Sheffield, in 1983. Whilst German-built engines were normally fitted to Setras, from 1991 agreement was reached with Scania to supply their engines and driveline for the new Series 300 coaches.

Smart and rather more restrained in style than the Neoplan equivalents is this double-deck coach on MAN chassis seen in Park Lane in June 1996.

This is an example of a Drögmöller integral coach. This factory from Heilbronn dated back to 1930 and was low volume, producing less than a hundred vehicles in 1983. The distinctive feature of their E series was the ramped floor with a matching bottom window line. This three-axle version was with a company from Kiel and was at Windsor in September 1997. Drögmöller were acquired by Volvo in 1994 but the loss-making factory closed in 2005 after a failed attempt to sell it to the Turkish coachbuilders Temsa.

This Neoplan Cityliner seen at Windsor in May 2008 is typical of the more exotic-looking designs from the company in the current century, and also of the more exotic liveries often now associated with German coaches. Neoplan have been a separate division of MAN since February 2008. There are plants in various countries including (formerly) in the United States.

Greece

This German-built Magirus Deutz, probably with Greek bodywork, was with a company from Athens. There is an impressive collection of travel stickers in the windscreen – has the vehicle actually visited all these places? Taken at King's Cross, August 1983.

A Volvo with Saracakis bodywork, parked outside Paddington station in August 1989.

Holland

DAF is a major vehicle manufacturer from Holland, established in 1928, originally making trailers. Bus and coach chassis production started in 1949. Components were also supplied to makers of integral vehicles including CBM and Van Hool. DAF and coachbuilders Bova formed the jointly owned company United Bus BV in 1990 to coordinate development, marketing and servicing. This venture collapsed in 1993. Since 2003 DAF has been part of VDL Bus & Coach. This coach with unknown bodywork was taken at St Paul's Cathedral in 1973 and came from Huurman, Bergschenhoek.

Taken at Brighton in May 1978, this is a Volvo with Verheul bodywork from Speedwell, Den Haag. Judging by the window sticker, it was probably there as a tender vehicle for a Dutch entry in the HCVS London–Brighton Historic Commercial Vehicle Run, taking place that day.

Seen at Bressendon Place, Victoria, in May 1977, this DAF of De Pelikaan, Breda has Van Hool bodywork.

On the same day, this DAF of Het Centrum, Lisse, has Smit C53F bodywork. Smit Autobusfabriek became part of the vast VDL Group.

This DAF taken in August 1979 had bodywork by Hainje. This was owned by a company called Beentjes en de Bruyn of Heemskerk and was liveried for De Jong Intratours. Hainje, who had 40 per cent of the Dutch city bus market in the 1980s, was taken over by Berkhof in 1989 but initially retained as a separate subsidiary until 1998. Their plant is now part of VDL Bus & Coach.

This DAF of Spectrum Reisen, Hoorn, taken in September 1979, had Bova bodywork. Bova of Eindhoven began coach production in 1931. Integral vehicles were built from 1969. Bova were taken over by the VDL Group in 2003, who by then also owned Berkhof and Jonckheere (of Belgium). They now trade as VDL Bova and are based at Valkenswaard.

At St Paul's in March 1980, this DAF has bodywork by Van Rooijen. Owned by Smits, Lith, it was liveried for Maaskant Tours duties. Alongside is a coach with Bova Europa bodywork – a style that attracted British customers.

This DAF of FSZ Reisen, Surhisterveen, seen in May 1981, has somewhat angular bodywork by Van Rooijen. Note how much higher this is than the Mercedes-Benz coach behind.

A high-floor body design by Berkhof was fitted to this Scania of Het Zuiden, Valkenburg, seen in July 1983. Judging from the lettering, it would seem that this company specialised in long-distance international tours so plenty of luggage space would have been available, as well as good visibility. Berkhof only started business in 1970 at Valkenswaald near Eindhoven. Berkhof bodies were supplied for the UK market by dealers Ensignbus with the first for Harwich & Dovercourt Coaches in 1982. Over 300 were sold to the UK in the 1980s including fifty-three for London Country Bus Services.

A DAF with unspecified bodywork, seen in April 1983. This was with Keller, Nieuwenhagen.

British coachbuilder Plaxton of Scarborough had some success in the European market and bodied a number of DAF SB series coaches for the Dutch market in the late 1970s/early 1980s. This pair was with Betuwe Express of Herveld at St Paul's in May 1985.

Photographed at the 1989 British Coach Rally, held that year at Southampton rather than Brighton, this coach of Jan Mekers, Etten, is a British-built Duple 425 integral, a model first unveiled at the 1984 Motor Show.

Smit bodywork was fitted to this coach of NZH Travel, seen at Hyde Park Corner in September 1995. NZH was a state-owned bus company in north-west Holland.

A Belgian-built LAG EOS coach for Peter Langhout Reisen, June 1996.

Hungary

The main manufacturer from Hungary was Ikarus. Typical of their products was this 256 model with Ibusz, Budapest, taken near St Paul's Cathedral in July 1981. The bunting is for the wedding of Prince Charles and Lady Diana Spencer, which took place at the cathedral on 29 July.

An Ikarus of Balatontourist at Windsor, June 1992. Ikarus had its origins in 1895. After Hungary became Communist the company was nationalised in 1948, although the Ikarus name was not adopted until 1951. They became the chief producer of buses for the Eastern Bloc. However, after the fall of Communism the company suffered and was eventually bought by the Irisbus Group, a joint venture of Iveco and Renault, in 1999 and the factory closed down in 2003. The company was sold back to Hungarian interests in 2006.

This unidentified coach was taken at Hyde Park Corner in March 2003.

Italy

Barbi bodywork was fitted to this Mercedes-Benz 0303 at St Paul's in August 1985.

Barbi bodywork was also fitted to this Iveco Fiat 370 of Garattini Reisen, taken at Gloucester Road in July 1984. Fiat became part of Iveco in 1975, which is now a multinational brand with factories in some sixteen countries across four continents.

Garbarini was the bodywork builder for this Scania 116 of Viaggi del Barba, seen in April 1984.

Fiat (Fabbrica Italiana Automobili di Torino) was founded in 1899, with commercial vehicles being produced from 1902. By 1906, double-deck buses, as well as trucks, were produced. This Fiat 370 was fitted with bodywork by Menarini and was taken in August 1982. Note the air-conditioning unit at the rear of the roof.

Menarini bodywork was also fitted to this coach, seen in August 1982.

Taken at Windsor in June 1982, this Mercedes-Benz 0303 has a Minerva L80 body. The owners were ASP of Perugia.

Pulling out of the coach park at St Paul's Cathedral in July 1981, this Fiat of Esitur has an Orlandi Poker body. Orlandi of Modena was a coachbuilding subsidiary of Fiat and then in turn Iveco.

At Gloucester Road in July 1981, this Mercedes-Benz 0302 has bodywork by Padane. This company operated from 1943 to 1992 and sold some bodies to UK operators.

Latvia

A Scandinavian combination of Volvo chassis with Ajokki bodywork seen in September 1995.

Luxembourg

Small country, big coach! An articulated Neoplan Transliner of Voyages Sales-Lentz at Olympia, May 1994.

Also from Luxembourg and seen alongside the articulated Neoplan at Olympia in May 1994 was this Setra double-deck coach of Voyages Emile Weber. An additional luggage locker can be seen attached to the rear of the coach.

Norway

Swedish chassis, Finnish bodywork. This Volvo has a Delta Plan Delta 400 body with forty-six seats. It was seen at St Paul's Cathedral, June 1982.

Same location in July 1983 and this Mercedes-Benz 0303 has bodywork by Føreland Karosserifabrikk A/S of Kristiansand. This was one of nine bus and coachbuilding companies operating in Norway during 1982. The coach was with Sola Ruten of Stavanger.

There is more of a dual-purpose look to this interesting Scania seen in April 1984. It was owned by Bergen-Nordhordland Rutelag and the bodywork was by Brodrene Repstad Karosserifabrikk of Søgne, seating forty-seven.

A three-axle Scania 116 with bodywork by Vest Karosseri A/S at Gloucester Road in July 1983. The owner was Nordfjord Og Sunnmore Billag from Stryn, where the body maker was based. The middle axle is non-powered and can be raised out of use. Vest-Buss was the largest bodybuilder in Norway by 2000 and in 2002 bought the former Leyland DAB plant at Silkeborg in Denmark from Scania ownership.

This Volvo B10M of Klæburuten, seen in September 1996, has Carrus bodywork. Carrus Oy was a Finnish company that was bought by Volvo in 1997 (see p. 20).

Poland

Polish-built coaches from Autosan (seen here) and Jelcz were exhibited on the Pol-Mot stand at the Motor Show held at the Birmingham National Exhibition Centre Commercial in October 1980. The Autosan H9-20 rear-engined coach with their own C41D bodywork had a Leyland 400 engine built under licence.

This Autosan was noted in Park Lane in May 1995. Autosan vehicles have been made at Sanuk since 1926.

This is a Jelcz, a Polish company founded in 1952. This was taken at St Paul's Cathedral in May 1994.

A similar vehicle but badged as a MAN in July 1999. Jelcz are still in business, but primarily as a maker of military vehicles so it would seem that the bus-building side was sold to MAN.

This is a TAM coach photographed at St Paul's in July 1981. TAM (Tovarna Avtomobilov Maribor) was founded in 1947 to build lorries at Maribor, Yugoslavia, which is now in Slovenia. The company went bankrupt in 2011 but has been restarted with Chinese investment and now specialises in buses and coaches.

This coach, of unknown make, was photographed parked on Park Lane in July 1992.

Bearing the very appropriate English name Visitor, this coach was parked near Victoria Coach Station in July 1997.

Portugal

Most of the vehicles from Portugal that I saw in the 1980s were from a tourist agency named Agência Abreu, based in Porto. No. 351 was a Volvo B10M with a raised rear section body by Camo. This was taken near Victoria in October 1982.

No. 353 of Abreu was another Volvo but with bodywork by Irmaos. This was seen at St Pancras in August 1983.

This Scania 112with Gaf bodywork, seen at Bayswater in August 1985, features a low driving position giving passengers a clear forward view.

Moving on to 1986 and No. 507 was a MAN with Portuguese bodywork by Caetano. This was taken at Gloucester Road.

Taken at Tower Hill in April 1988, this Volvo was owned by Camara Municipal de Alcanena. The body on this was by Cartejo.

This is a MAN with Caetano body, seen in April 1995.

This Volvo B10MT with Camo Mirage high-deck bodywork was entered in the trade display at the 1990 British Coach Rally held at Southampton in April 1990. Camo was founded in Ourense, Spain, in 1995 but also has a plant in Porto. Over 80 per cent of production is exported.

Romania

This Scania has bodywork by Ghabbour, a company from Cairo, Egypt, which was founded in 1960. The resemblance to a Duple Dominant design is no accident – Ghabbour assembled body kits supplied by Duple Metsec. This was taken in August 1996.

Slovakia

This MAN coach of Satur was photographed in June 2004.

Spain

A 1960s Setra fitted with an air-conditioning unit mounted on the roof. Alongside, TUD 179L of Heyfordian Coaches is an example of a Portuguese-built Caetano body for a British operator, probably on a Bedford chassis. Taken in 1975, this site, opposite the Old Vic Theatre at Waterloo, was used for coach parking at the time but has since been landscaped as a garden area.

Iberbus No. 71 was a Pegaso 5031L with Ayats bodywork, which was parked near Victoria in September 1982. In 1990 Iveco bought a majority shareholding in the Spanish state-owned manufacturer Enasa, the parent company of Pegaso.

Ayats Olimpo double-deck coachwork was fitted to this coach of Pujol & Pujol, visiting Windsor in 1991. Ayats is a long-established family firm founded in 1905 and based at Abrucies, near Girona. Their recent bodies have been characterised by large amounts of glass at the front.

Seen at Windsor in September 1981, this Pegaso has bodywork by Beulas, a company still in business in 2023.

Owned by F. Sainz de la Maza, Bilbao, this Pegaso had dual-door bodywork by Camelsa. Note the sliding windows rather than fixed windows and air conditioning, more common on Spanish coaches. June 1982.

With St Pancras station hotel in the background, this Mercedes-Benz 0303 had a Camelsa C52D body. June 1983.

This Pegaso, seen in July 1983, had bodywork by Cilsac.

The small red badge on the front grille of this coach reads 'Leyland Iberica', so was this a Leyland Leopard or a Spanish-built coach fitted with a Leyland engine? The C47D coachwork was by Icarsa. Owned by Imperio S. I. Autocares, it was seen at Gloucester Road in July 1981.

This Pegaso 5031L of Jai-Alai, Ondarroa, was fitted with a raised rear-section C57D body by Icarsa. Seen in April 1982. Icarsa was the trading name of Castro Carrocera, who were taken over in 1998 by Carrocera Castrosua from Santiago de Compostela, who were still in business in 2023.

At Gloucester Road in August 1980, this Mercedes-Benz 0302 has bodywork by Irizar. Irizar remains as a major coachbuilding company, supplying bodies and integrals to operators across Europe and beyond.

Laying over at Battersea in October 1984, this Pegaso is liveried in the colours of the Spanish national railway system RENFE. The make of bodywork is unknown.

Sunsundegui bodywork is now a common sight in the UK, but this Spanish company only began building coaches in 1987. Founded in 1944, they had previously been engaged in repairing rolling stock for RENFE, the Spanish rail company. They moved into a new factory at Alsasua in 2017 and now over 85 per cent of production is exported. This is the Stylo model, the second design from the company, and this was seen mounted on a Mercedes-Benz 0404 coach at Windsor in 1997.

This Pegaso with Unicar bodywork was laying over at Windsor in September 1978, in the same year this style of bodywork began to be imported into Britain (see p. 91). Union Carrocera, or Unicar, came from Catoira in Galicia.

Sweden

I came across this rather fierce-looking old Scania-Vabis bus at Gloucester Road in July 1984. It was being used as transport for a theatre group. It presumably formerly served at Vaxholm, an island archipelago city near Stockholm.

This coach, presumably a Scania or Volvo, although not badged, was photographed in Westminster during July 1974. The forty-three-seat body was by Autokori. Note the pair of front seats, ahead of the door, which appear to face inwards towards the driver rather than forwards. The owners were Erlandssons Trafik AB.

A Scania with Finnish-built Ajokki C53D coachwork at St Paul's in June 1977. This was with Kalmar Omnibusförening. Scania began in 1900 and merged with Vabis (founded in 1891) in 1911. Bus production began in 1920. The Vabis part of the name was dropped in 1968.

A later style of Ajokki body, the 9000 Superstar model on a Scania K112 of Sennans Buss in 1986.

Similar style coachwork, but now badged as Delta Plan. This Scania with Sjöbo Buss was taken in Park Lane in 1992. The first British operator to buy a Delta Plan body was Kettlewell of Retford, who took A50 WVL, a two-axle Scania K112, in 1984.

Rather interestingly, this Scania 116 of Bussapågarna, Staffanstorp, has bodywork by Ikarus of Hungary. From 1976, Sweden ordered a number of bodies from Ikarus, modified to fit Swedish regulations and mounted on Scandinavian chassis. The design was known as the Ikarus 194 and production continued until 1987. July 1983.

This Volvo B10M of Smålands Bussen was fitted with coachwork by Wiima of Finland. Note the Swedish flag painted on the front. St Paul's Cathedral, April 1987. Volvo (Latin for 'I roll') was founded in 1915 originally as a subsidiary of the ball-bearing maker SKF and truck production began in 1928.

Switzerland

This Mercedes-Benz 0303 with unknown but probably German bodywork was taken in Glasgow during July 1999.

Turkey

Coaches from Turkey were quite a rarity. This is a Mercedes-Benz 0302 with Otomarsan coachwork at Gloucester Road in August 1980. Otomarsan was established in Istanbul in 1967 to manufacture Mercedes-Benz vehicles. The company became Mercedes-Benz Turk A.S. in 1990.

Seen in April 1998, this is a Mitsubishi. The European manufacturer's dominance of the European market was starting to be challenged by Japanese and later Chinese competition.

'Unknown'

I photographed this coach heading down Whitehall in August 1995, but was never able to establish which country it was from. It is probably from part of former Communist Eastern Europe as the vehicle is a Slovenian-built TAM. The fleet name was the very English 'Street Tour'.

Hotel Coaches

Rotel Tours of Passau, Germany, had a fleet of around 150 hotel coaches by 2000. They came in two types. One version, like this Mercedes-Benz 0303, had three tiers of bunk beds in the rear section of the coach. This was taken outside Madame Tussauds in Marylebone Road, August 2001. Their other variant was a conventional coach (though with roof luggage rack), which towed a trailer that opened out into sleeping berths. Economy was probably a higher consideration than comfort.

This MAN coach with a German operator taken at Windsor in June 1992 shows the small curtained windows of the sleeping berths and has a separate entrance door to the sleeping compartment.

Based on a Van Hool integral, this was operated by a company from Aachen, Germany, and was towing a luggage trailer. Photographed passing St Paul's, April 1995.

This example from Belgium has a Jonckheere body. Park Lane, London, July 1991.

This MAN, seen on the Embankment near Charing Cross in July 1996, came from a company in the Czech Republic calling itself Aqua Club. These hotel coaches were licensed under local country rules, but new EU rules on safety and overall length came into effect in the 2000s, which largely ended their use in member countries. Germany was planning to ban them altogether in 2005.

International Coach Services

The opening of the Channel Tunnel with direct Eurostar trains to Paris and Brussels alongside the development of budget airlines killed off most of the services to Western Europe. However, other services emerged as the influx of workers from former Communist Eastern European states increased.

Before the advent of through coach services to Europe, East Kent was operating coaches that connected with ferry or hovercraft sailings. DJG 617C, a 1965 AEC Reliance with Park Royal C49F body, is liveried for the Hoverlloyd service from Ramsgate to Calais, with connections on to Paris. This was at Victoria Coach Station on 21 April 1972.

Europabus began services to London in 1975. This Mercedes-Benz 0302 of Deutsche Touring Gesellschaft, Frankfurt, was taken in Victoria Coach Station on 12 July 1975.

Another Europabus service, but this is from Brussels to London and a Belgian-owned Setra S140 laying over at Battersea in August 1978.

A through service between London and Galway in Ireland began on 23 May 1975, jointly worked by National Travel (North West) and the Irish state operator Coras Iompair Eireann. CIE WVH13, one of twenty 1963 Leyland Royal Tiger Worldmaster ERT2/1 coaches rebodied by Van Hool in 1970, stands at Victoria Coach Station on 12 July 1975. This coach had had its gear ratios modified to allow for UK motorway running at speeds higher than the Irish maximum.

CIE MD202 at Battersea on 21 June 1981. This was a Leyland Leopard PSU5/4R with CIE C48F bodywork, painted in the Expressway red/yellow livery. It has come from Limerick, crossing from Rosslare to Pembroke.

Also at Battersea, this time in July 1982, is CIE KE6, also in Expressway livery. CIE had stopped buying Leylands and were now buying these Irish-built Bombardier-GM integral buses and coaches with Bombardier bodies and General Motors Detroit Diesel engines. This is a dual-purpose model with DP45F seating, dating from 1981.

Another CIE Bombardier-GM TC, but KE48, also dating from 1981, is painted in coach livery and has curtains fitted. Note also the absence of a blind box as this has been designated for touring duties. This was also at Battersea on the service from Limerick in April 1984. The body designs were by a German consultancy and the idea was to have common windows and some other parts for both double- and single-deck buses and coaches for maximum interchangeability.

CIE MD27, a 1971 Leyland Leopard PSU5/4R with CIE C53F bodywork, in the coach livery at Battersea in July 1985. Some of these Leylands had been rebuilt with GM engines (MG class), whilst others like this had been given DAF engines (MD class).

In 1986 CIE bought EVH 1–15, Van Hool Acron T815 integrals with Cummins L10 engines. EVH 12 is at Battersea and carries the Expressway livery applied to these.

National Travel South East acquired OYT 529–32R in 1976. These were left-hand-drive AEC Reliances with Willowbrook C47F bodies specifically for use on European express services. OYT 530R was exhibited at the Brighton Coach Rally in 1977. It was reported in *Buses* magazine that these had originally been intended as an export order for an operator in Nigeria that was cancelled. Note that both National and Europabus symbols are carried.

This French Saviem has worked over from Paris with a 'Magic Bus' budget service, probably aimed at the student and backpacker market. It was laying over at what is now the site of the British Library in Euston Road, February 1981. Magic Bus linked up with National Express on bookings and marketing but the company collapsed in December 1982. It was replaced by a new European division of National Express named Supabus from May 1983. From April 1986 most Anglo-European services were marketed as Eurolines UK. This became a separate company within National Express in 1989.

Articulated 'bendy-coaches' were a feature found in Europe but not legal in Britain until the early 1980s. This Van Hool coach with Fiat running units was with Bovo Tours of Roleofarendsveen. This was being used at the time on the Amsterdam–London Magic Bus international express service and had taken time out between services to appear at the London Bus Rally held at the depot of Ensignbus, Purfleet, in July 1982. However, in September 1982 such vehicles were banned from the outside lane of British motorways and their use on these services ended.

In June 1985 the National Bus Company set up a new operating and marketing company named Voyage National, based in Lille in northern France. It was 70 per cent British owned and 30 per cent French owned. This French-registered Volvo B10M/Jonckheere P50 coach was photographed laying over outside Victoria Coach Station and was one of three delivered when the company started. The company was sold off in 1987 as part of the privatisation of the National Bus Company.

Sadem, Italy, 286, an Iveco, at Battersea in 1983 having arrived on a Euroways service from Rome via Paris. Note that this carries both Fiat and Iveco badging.

Iberbus of Spain ran a service from Algeciras via Madrid. Also seen at Battersea, this time in August 1984, is an Ayats Apollo-bodied Pegaso. The low driving position was achieved by inserting a drop section in the front end of the chassis with the approval of the chassis manufacturer. The first British customer was Sunshine Holidays of Coventry in 1982. Another coach with this bodywork was exhibited at the 1982 Motor Show, destined for Hogg, Boston, Lincolnshire. They were produced on Magirus Deutz chassis as Pegaso did not have a UK presence.

Arriving at Victoria Coach Station on 29 July 1982, this Irizar Urko-bodied Pegaso of Julia, Spain, has worked through from Alicante via Barcelona.

Parra, San Adrian, 19, NA-3025-L, a Scania 116 with bodywork by Obradors, at Victoria in August 1982. This has a board attached stating that it has arrived on the Iberbus Alicante–Madrid–Paris–London service.

GDG Continentbus of Sweden ran a route to Stockholm for Europabus. This Volvo/Van Hool was promoting the service with an appearance at the rally held at London Transport's Chiswick Works on 3 July 1983 to mark fifty years of London Transport.

A later vehicle with Deutsche Touring, this is a Belgian-built LAG EOS integral parked outside Victoria Coach Station in August 1992. The sign in the windscreen reads 'Munchen–Frankfurt–Brussel–London'. LAG were taken over by Van Hool in June 1990, although this model continued to be built at the LAG factory in Bree.

A Mercedes-Benz from Polish company Bermuda reaches journey's end arriving at Victoria on a scheduled service from Poland in January 2005.

A MAN from the Czech Republic arriving at Victoria on an express service in September 2008.

Early Foreign-built Coaches with British Operators

There were a number of imported coach chassis in the earlier part of the twentieth century, particularly before the Bedford range became established and started to dominate the lightweight end of the British market. This 1929 Chevrolet LQ with Spicer C14D bodywork was new to Jardine (White Heather), Morecambe, and is now preserved by the Lincolnshire Vintage Vehicle Society. Seen at Brighton in 1984.

Bodywork by Salvador Caetano from Portugal was first marketed in Britain by dealers Alf Moseley as the 'Moseley Continental' in 1968. This 1970 Lisboa model was fitted on an AEC Reliance chassis for Bonas (Supreme Coaches), Coventry, seen in Coventry in 1971.

Glenn Valley, London, SE22, was operating this rare example of a Bedford VAL with Caetano Estoril bodywork, OKX 234H, when photographed arriving at the Epsom Derby in June 1981. These Caetano bodies had steel framing at a time when British Duple and Plaxton bodies still used timber framing.

This Bedford YRT with Caetano Estoril body was seen at Southampton Docks awaiting delivery to the operator in March 1973 and not yet registered. It would become HOM 471L with Bowen, Birmingham.

The 'Moseley Continental' branding can be seen above the front wheel on this 1973 Bedford VAS5 with C29F body for R & I Tours of London seen in 1974. Since 2006 Salvador Caetano have become the main choice of coachbuilder by National Express for supply to their contracted operators.

Van Hool of Koningshooikt, Belgium, broke through into Ireland ahead of the UK market with bodies on some new Leyland Leopards, one of which was exhibited at the Earls Court Commercial Motor Show in 1970, and some rebodied Royal Tiger Worldmasters (see p. 76). WUR 865K was a 1972 Bedford YRQ with a Van Hool C45F body in the fleet of Southern Motorways. This was taken at Winchester in August 1973.

An entry in the British Coach Rally at Brighton in 1977 was Best Tours, London, VUR 227K, an AEC Reliance/Van Hool Vistadome executive coach with just twenty-eight seats and fitted toilet. This had previously been entered at both the Brighton and Blackpool coach rallies when new in 1972 and had been the outright winner at both events.

Probably the first foreign-bodied coach for a National Bus Company fleet was NUK 561K. This 1972 Ford R226 with Van Hool C32F body with National Travel Midlands had been acquired with the takeover of Don Everall, Wolverhampton, in 1974, who had also been dealers marketing Van Hool products. Seen at Battersea in June 1978.

World Wide Coaches, London, was one of the first British companies to take the Mercedes-Benz 0302 integral and bought the largest amount of the thirty-six imported with fifteen taken between 1971 and 1973. LGY 193K is seen here on tour at Winchester on 29 September 1973. World Wide later became part of the Ewer Group and the 0302s were sold off soon after.

World Wide also took one of the seventeen underframes imported and this was fitted with a one-off Plaxton Panorama Elite III body. Taken at Heathrow in 1975, ONK 657H had been entered in the British Coach Rally at Brighton in 1970 and 1973.

Mid-Warwickshire Motors NAC 276L, a 1973 AEC Reliance with Jonckheere bodywork, seen arriving at Wembley Stadium in March 1978. This was acquired with the business of Shirleys Coaches, Meriden, and sometimes used on that former operator's Meriden – Solihull stage service.

A rare model was the AEC/UTIC. UTIC was a cooperative venture set up by Portuguese bus operators to make vehicles for the home market. Around 1970 they designed an integral fifty-three-seat coach with a rear-mounted AEC AH691 engine. Following their success with Caetano bodywork, the Moseley Group imported this design to Britain marketed as the Tagus. However, with the then British suspicion of integral coaches, only nine were sold in a three-year period. Seen arriving at Wembley in May 1975, GDU 66L was one of a pair new to Bonas, Coventry, in 1972. This had passed to Bowen, Birmingham, in 1974.

On show at the Southsea Rally in June 1976, this Bus & Car Eagle C48Ft coach built in Belgium was running on trade plates. The demonstrator was liveried and supposedly destined for Tatlock's, Bury, and the UK importing agent was based in Portsmouth, hence its appearance. It had previously been displayed at the Scottish Motor Show in November 1975. This vehicle featured a rear-mounted Detroit V8 two-stroke engine developing 280 bhp, air conditioning and a toilet. It retailed for a then massive £43,000, more than twice the price for a Bedford. None were sold.

The first coach for a British operator with Spanish-built Ayats bodywork was this 1975 Leyland Leopard PSU5/4R with David Corbel of Edgware. This was parked outside Embankment station in August 1976. The 12-metre coach had fifty-seven seats and was entered in the1975 British Coach Rally at Brighton. This would remain a one-off, and Ayats sold only three more coaches to the UK into the early 1980s, all on Magirus Deutz chassis.

Another Spanish coachbuilder competing for the British market was Unicar. This as yet unregistered Bedford YMT was destined for Kings Ferry, Lidsing, when first displayed at the 1978 British Coach Rally. As with Caetano, Moseley were the dealers importing these. Over 100 bodies were acquired in 1979–80, mostly on Bedford YMT or Volvo B58 chassis, plus one on a Ford R1114 chassis. One Bedford, EBC 567T, has been reacquired by original owners Winson, Loughborough, for preservation after later service in Malta.

Also competing in a big way was Volvo with the B58 chassis, the first UK examples going to Golden Miller of Feltham in 1973. This Volvo B58/Plaxton C53F coach for Hills, Tredegar, was an entry at the 1976 British Coach Rally at Brighton. An earlier model, PWO 412M, had been entered in 1974.

From 1976, DAF started to compete for the British chassis market with their first sale to Robinson's, Appleby. A MB200DKL model with Van Hool 300 series C49F body for Mitcham Belle was exhibited in the demonstration park at the 1976 Commercial Motor Show at Earls Court. It was a sign of the times that in 1979 this DAF with a Van Hool C30Ft executive coach body was awarded Coach of the Year at the British Coach Rally, Brighton. Owned by David Fox, Middlesbrough, this was photographed at Wembley in 1980. This style of Van Hool body, the Aragon range, was made at their factory in Spain.

European imports, both chassis and bodywork, were also impacting on the midicoach market from the 1970s. ELB 165T, R&I Tours, London, was a truck-derived Fiat 55F10 chassis with a body by Harwin Coachbuilders of Liverpool. This was taken in 1981.

Fourteen Volvo B58-61 coaches were imported to the UK in 1979–81 with stepped-roof Irizar Urko bodies. The first went to Trathens of Yelverton, Devon, and UJY 456V is seen when nearly new in Leeds.

The MAN SR280 integral coach was first offered in Great Britain when a new marketing company MAN-VW Truck & Bus Ltd was set up in 1979 to market the commercial vehicle products of MAN and Volkswagen. A demonstrator was shown at the 1979 Brighton Coach Rally. One of the first operators of the type was Angela Coaches, Burseldon, Hampshire, in 1979 with a 12-metre executive coach (GPA 609V) to provide transport for the Southampton football team. This was one of five more that followed in 1981. By the end of 1982 over ninety SR280s had been bought by British companies.

Kässbohrer Setra was another German manufacturer of integral coaches who were making inroads into the British market. Their first customer was Kirbys of Rayleigh, Essex, who bought an S130 model registered OTW 116K in 1971. This HD215 coach for the operator was an exhibit at the 1980 Motor Show, held at the Birmingham National Exhibition Centre, and featured a Mercedes-Benz engine.

In 1980 Ensign became the importing agents for Italian coachbuilder Padane. The first sold was a ZX body on ADR 200W, a 1980 Mercedes-Benz 0303 for Trathens, Yelverton. A second 0303 came in 1981, NFJ 369W, with a lower height Z body. This is seen at Gloucester Road in March 1984 when re-registered 602 LTT. In 1982 Trathens took seven Padane ZX bodies on Volvo B10M chassis. Ensign had a demonstrator built on a Leyland Tiger chassis but these ten coaches would be the only UK examples.

Trathens were also the first British operator of the Neoplan Skyliner when they bought two in 1981 for their Plymouth–Exeter–London service operated in collaboration with National Express. Another early British customer for the Neoplan Skyliner was Ebdons of Sidcup. EFW 863X was passing St Paul's Cathedral on 25 August 1983. They would go on to buy several further examples over the next decade. From 1984 Neoplan Skyliners were available with a British-made Gardner engine as an alternative to the standard Mercedes unit.

Wallace Arnold turned to European coaches in 1982, cancelling an order for ten Leyland Tigers and buying twelve Bova Europa integrals (a design introduced to Britain in 1981) and four Setra S6216H integrals. One of the Bova coaches is seen at Battersea in January 1983 lettered for the Rapide service from Yorkshire to London developed initially under the British Coachways banner and by now run in collaboration with National Express. Indeed, vehicles on this service would later be painted in National Express Rapide livery but with the Wallace Arnold name.

A Jonckheere-bodied DAF of Derek Randall, London, in 1982. In 1983 this company would make the first major British order for Scania coaches after their introduction to the market in 1982. They bought fifteen of the new K112 chassis, also fitted with Jonckheere bodies. These were used on tour work to the south of France, Spain and Austria. Another fifteen came in 1984 but the company collapsed in September 1985.

Only three coaches by the former German company Drögmöller were sold in the UK and this 1984 E330 Comet with ramped floor is the sole survivor. Previously registered B484 MLN, this was displayed at the 1984 Motor Show with a price tag of £100,000. This was bought by Bergland, Watford, who later also bought two E320 Euro-Pullmans with flat floors. It is now part of the heritage fleet of G. H. Watts Coaches, Leicester, and was an exhibit at Showbus, Duxford, in 2009.